I'd give you a nasty look, but you've already got one

All of these flavours, and you choose to be salty

It must be so much easier when you don't have to think things through

Unlike the stomach, the brain doesn't know when it's empty

That's tempting to therapise

Does your arsehole get jealous of the shit that comes out of your mouth?

An empty vessel makes the loudest noise

Try not to think too often, you will only hurt yourself

Is this the same brain you use to cross the street? Talk about living on the edge

You're not a bottleneck, you're more like a scenic route with roadworks

Did you come up with that all on your own?
I thought I could smell something burning

Other than the obvious, what would you change about yourself?

You haven't been burdened with an overabundance of schooling have you?

Your ideas have a lot of... potential for further discussion

I can explain it to you, but I can't understand it for you

Look, I don't know what your problem is, but I bet it's hard to pronounce

I wish I could tell you how much I enjoyed this

One of your finer qualities is that no thought ever goes unspoken

I didn't mean to push all of your buttons, I was just looking for mute

Your determination to convince me that you know what you're talking about is impressive

As far as intellectual luggage is concerned, you are travelling light

I want you to know that I personally have no problem with you being here

How do you not fall down more often?

I'd feel real dumb if I said that out loud

You have something in your teeth

I could eat a bowl of alphabet soup and shit out a smarter statement than whatever you just said

That's what people who don't know anything about it always say

I get so emotional when you are not around

That emotion is happiness

I'm not insulting you

I'm describing you

Keep rolling your eyes, you might eventually find a brain

It's impossible to underestimate you

If I wanted to hear from an arsehole, I would fart

You fear success, but you really have nothing to worry about

Do you want a cape, so you can be super annoying?

You don't waste time on nuance, do you? Very efficient

Well, aren't you just a cookie full of arsenic

As an outsider, what is your opinion on the topic of intelligence?

You have a talent for sounding informed while remaining refreshingly void of the facts

You have clearly reached a conclusion and spared yourself the inconvenience of doubt

Nice Shoes!
Who tied them?

I'm sorry, my vocabulary fails me. I can't think of a single way to respond to you that doesn't come off as condescending, sarcastic and disrespectful

I'm sorry, you seem upset. Is it because of your haircut?

One has to respect your enthusiasm, if nothing else

I love how you commit fully to ideas without letting research interfere

You have a firm grasp on the obvious

The bar was set on the ground and you bought a shovel

I'm sure you couldn't have done any better if you tried

I can see the limits of your comprehension have been met

You could hide your own Easter eggs

I see your antennas don't pick up all of the channels

You are three standard deviations below the mean

I know you tried your best and that's what is so disappointing

I thought you were a halfwit; I now see that was wildly optimistic

You're as bright as a two-watt lightbulb

You are proof that effort and results aren't always related

Everyone starts somewhere.
I guess some people just stay there

I'll never forget the first time we met, but I'll keep trying

You have delusions of adequacy

Here is a tissue, you have a little bullshit on your lip

I hope you go far, the sooner the better

Don't study me. You won't graduate

You talk so much shit, I don't know whether to offer you a breath mint or toilet paper

Of course I talk like an idiot, how else would you understand me?

Isn't it dangerous to use your whole vocabulary in one sentence?

I love how you state the obvious with such a sense of discovery

When I look into your eyes, I get the feeling someone else is driving

May the both sides of your pillow be uncomfortably warm

You display all the wisdom of a poorly translated proverb

I can't tell you have much I have enjoyed this conversation

You are the Monday of my life

You only have two brain cells and they are both fighting for third place

Don't be ashamed of who you are, that's your parent's job

I envy everyone you've never met

One of the few people who can add something to a room by leaving it

You are the human version of period cramps

You have a special way of speaking which makes people appreciate your silence

You're about as useful as an ashtray on a motorcycle

You speak with the authority of experience and the accuracy of assumption

You are a gray sprinkle on a rainbow cupcake

That is a very unique way to think about that... ever find anyone who agrees?

You must have been born on a highway.

That's where most accidents happen

Some people wonder if you are an idiot, then you open your mouth and remove all doubt

It's okay if you don't like me, not everyone has good taste!

You approached that with the precision of a blindfolded archer

Are you a black Friday sale? because I'm wondering what your deal is!

Wisdom has always been chasing you, but you have always been faster

I'd agree with you, but then we would both be wrong

I love what you have done with your hair!

How do you get it to come out of your nostrils like that

www.ingramcontent.com/pod-product-compliance
Lightning Source LLC
Chambersburg PA
CBHW031309060426
42444CB00033B/1094